Peter Pitseolak's Escape from Death

Published in the United States by
Delacorte Press/Seymour Lawrence,
245 East 47th Street, New York City 10017

ISBN: 0-440-06894-0
Library of Congress catalog card number: 77-83236

Design: Peter Dorn
Printing: Herzig Somerville Limited

A film strip version of *Peter Pitseolak's Escape from
Death* exists in ''The Arctic through Eskimo Eyes,''
a series of four film strips produced by International
Cinemedia Center, Ltd., Toronto, copyright © 1975.

A HARLEY EBER PRODUCTION

Printed in Canada

Drawings and story by Peter Pitseolak

Peter Pitseolak's Escape from Death

Introduced and edited by Dorothy Eber

j P487p

A Merloyd Lawrence Book
Delacorte Press/Seymour Lawrence

For Ashevak

About the text

Peter Pitseolak wrote two accounts in Eskimo syllabics – the system of writing based on shorthand brought north by the missionaries – of his and his stepson Ashevak's narrow escape, and the story as it appears here draws passages from both. Translation of the original manuscripts was by Eva Keleotak Deer and Lucy Carrière.

Acknowledgments

Special thanks to
The Canada Council for generous assistance
The West Baffin Eskimo Co-operative for its loan of original drawings.

Introduction

Although this true adventure in the arctic waters is a story of present-day Eskimo life, Peter Pitseolak is known on Baffin Island as the southwest Baffin Eskimos' own historian. Earlier than many, he knew that the Eskimo way of life was disappearing and when I met him in 1971 he had the habit of "writing down what happens from day to day so my grandchildren will know what went on while I was alive." In 1973, the last year of his life, we worked together on a book illustrated with his own photographs, which told "of the doings of the Eskimo people" and life on Baffin Island – his "giant island, lovely land."

His marvelous half-sister, Eleeshushee, well into her eighties when I met her, once told me, not altogether approvingly, how Peter Pitseolak came to know so much. "When we were children and the grown-ups were talking on the snow platform in the igloo, they would send the children away. But Peter Pitseolak would stay. He would turn his head and pretend not to be listening, but he was listening all the time!"

Peter Pitseolak had, indeed, a lot to tell.

He was born in 1902, and during his lifetime the missionaries, the traders, the law, the government, schools, and alcohol came to Baffin Island. But at the time of his birth the forces of change were still in their infancy. Some relatives worked for the whalers active in the Hudson Strait, and Peter Pitseolak's father and grandfather, both powerful leaders, were among the first to have guns. But essentially Peter Pitseolak lived in his childhood the same nomadic camp life his ancestors knew.

The picture changed as he grew up. When he was about eleven years old, hunters of the southwest Baffin coast built a giant beacon on a headland to guide the ships of the fur traders into Cape Dorset. The Hudson's Bay Company built a fur-trade post there, and the hunters became trappers, trading their skins for the white man's goods.

Shortly after the traders came, when Peter Pitseolak was still a young boy, his father died, and for a time he knew what it was to feel like a poor relation. Once he showed me his collection of guns. It covered a wall in his house. When he was learning to hunt, he had to make do with decrepit weapons, and he promised himself that when he was "able to afford things" he would have the best guns he could buy. He became a rich and powerful hunter. He was a right-hand man to the traders; he owned his own hunting boats; he was boss of Keatuk, the camp where ten families lived under his leadership; he had two trapping areas and twenty dogs – enough for two teams. When I met him, he was known throughout Baffin Island – a man with great drive, some faults – he had a hot temper – and remarkable qualities of mind and heart.

Today Cape Dorset is a large settlement, home to the families who in the sixties still had permanent camps in Seekooseelak – the name means "where there is no ice at break-up." ("Other coasts have a great deal," Peter Pitseolak used to explain.) Nowadays the camps are still loved and visited, but no one lives full time on the land. Children have to go to school, and for most people hunting is a part-time occupation.

Peter Pitseolak belonged, of course, to the first generation of his people with the means to leave a permanent record. (He sometimes seemed a bit unforgiving towards his forebears: "We were stupid," he once declared, "we should have thought of writing on sealskins.") He himself used every means of communication that came to hand. In his childhood the missionaries brought reading and writing – he learned the ABCs from songs the missionaries sang – and much later he owned tape recorders and cameras. His photographs captured the last days of Eskimo camp life, and were developed with the help of his remarkable wife, Aggeok, in igloo, tent and hut. And as the pictures in this book indicate, he also used other powerful means of communication – painting and drawing.

Peter Pitseolak did his first paintings in 1939 for an Englishman he called "Johanassie" Buchan, who was the son of the famous Lord Tweedsmur, Canada's Governor General at the time. During his father's term of office, Johanassie – or John Buchan, now the second Lord Tweedsmuir – worked at the trading post in Cape Dorset.

In letters he has recalled how the paintings, now in the National Museum of Man, Ottawa, came to be: "My mother had given me a sketch block and a paint box.

I was sitting in the post one winter's day, trying to paint a picture of the other side of the harbor and the pale glow of winter sunlight, when Pitseolak came along and asked me what I was doing.

"I explained to him that I was trying to put the winter sun down on paper. After some thought he said that what I was putting down didn't seem to him to resemble the sky. Rather testily, I replied that he was welcome to try and do better himself, and gave him the paint box and block. He brought the block back in the summer with every page covered with the most remarkable paintings."

Peter Pitseolak had no lessons in perspective. But like an early Renaissance painter, he worked out his own rules. He could do it, says Johanassie Buchan, "because he was a genius."

The pictures that illustrate this story were done when Peter Pitseolak and I were working together on the book called *People from our side.* This was a record of the old ways in his own words and photographs. It was published two years after his death. Originally we planned to include this story in the book, along with one or two illustrations. But when I received Peter Pitseolak's sixteen brilliant small drawings, it was clear they deserved a book of their own.

The pictures are reproduced here in actual size, along with four larger drawings by Peter Pitseolak that complement the story. All are done with felt pen, crayon or pencil, sometimes all three.

In the region where this story takes place, the Eskimo people know of many tragedies and miraculous escapes from the days when they hunted from skin boats. Peter Pitseolak and Ashevak wore "kadluna" clothing – the white man's clothes – and hunted from a modern "canoe," as Cape Dorset people call their outboard motor boats. But arctic waters and ice floes are no less dangerous for modern hunters.

Peter Pitseolak's Escape from Death is a story of men against the elements and – depending on your point of view – the luck or divine assistance that brings them home.

Dorothy Harley Eber
Montreal, 1977

This is a true story I'm telling and drawing of how I, Peter Pitseolak, went walrus hunting and almost didn't come home to my wife and children and grandchildren.

It happened off Seekooseelak – the coast where there is no ice at break-up. That's the Eskimo name for our land – southwest Baffin Island on the Hudson Strait.

It was a beautiful day to go hunting.
My son Ashevak was with me but there
were no other canoes. I didn't want to be
only one canoe on the water and I told
people, "We ought to think of hunting
some walrus while the weather is nice."
But everyone else was busy.

Ashevak and I put the fuel in our outboard
canoe and pushed off.

We wanted to reach a place where the walrus lie in the sun and take naps for many hours. When we got near I looked all around us with the telescope but at first I didn't see anything – the sun was directly in our eyes. Then my son saw them! But by that time one walrus had already smelled us and dived. We had to hurry to reach them before they all went under water.

While we were still quite far away I fired
but I missed. At that moment they all dived
into the sea. We followed them in the boat
and we shot three. Then we harpooned
them to keep them floating.

I do not draw every single thing – it would
take too long – but this is how Ashevak
and I killed walrus that day we were blown
out of sight of land.

One walrus was really big. Even Ashevak
and I together could not haul it onto the
ice. My son had to cut all the gut out of
it before we could pull it out of the water.

It got dark as we cut the walrus into
pieces. Once we heard the sound of other
canoes, their motors fading toward the
land. I lit a cloth and put it on top of my
harpoon and ran around with it. We hoped
that the people in the canoes would see
us and come and help us with the meat.
But nobody saw our light.

The moon was up when we finally finished with the meat. We started our canoe but it started badly. There was only a little noise coming from the motor. Right away we were suspicious it would break.

My son was looking at the motor so intently he did not see me wave and we bumped into ice. Soon our motor stopped completely.

Ashevak tried to fix it but he had no luck. It did not start again.

During the night a very strong wind came up. I have always feared the wind. This wind began moving us far from where we had started, out of sight of land. We could do nothing. I was always a driving man, one who gave orders, but I knew now I was no stronger than anyone else.

When morning came we found we were close to a very big ice field. It was moving towards us fast, brought by a swift current. We were very scared. We tried to get away but we were too slow. We could do nothing.

Soon we were in the middle of the ice field. The current was moving us fast down the Hudson Strait.

We pulled our canoe up on the ice.
We could only stay there and drift with
the current.

My son kept trying to fix our motor.
He started it; it was going but then it broke
again. We were so disappointed when
it broke that time. Ashevak kept working
at it but I knew he could not fix it. I got
very sad thinking about how our children
and grandchildren would ask when we
were coming back. I thought about how
our families would look for us and never
find us.

When we couldn't seem to do anything
I thought of a hymn and we sang it so
that our spirits would have a nice place
to be after we were dead. I am not trying
to be anyone special but that's what we
did when we thought we were going to die.
We said a prayer.

The second night on the ice I had a strange
dream.

There were creatures, demons,
strange spirits.

Then a bird came to me. It was a blue bird. It spoke to me in English. This bird of my dream said, "Hold to my neck and I'll fly you to safety." It took us on its back, one by one, to the shore. This dream was so real; I really believed my dream.

When I woke up I told my dream to Ashevak
and we started to get ready to move.

We left our oil drums and our motor in order to lighten the load and began to pull the canoe. But we were very tired and soon we had to stop for a rest. We had some of our walrus meat and then I said to my son, "Wake me up when you see a path in the ice." I said this because I believed there would be a path.

At midnight he woke me. A path had
opened up and we had the moon to guide
us. The wind had changed and it drove
us forward. All my life I had hated the wind
but now it was taking us to safety. There
is nothing in the world that is not good.
I understood this then.

At first the path was narrow but it broad-
ened out. Suddenly Ashevak became very
excited. I looked and saw the largest white
whale I have ever seen in my life. That
whale was enormous! We were scared
for the canoe. But it moved under the ice
and didn't show up again.

In the morning we were in open water.
We could see Baffin Island. That night before
midnight we came to shore near where
Sakiassie has his camp. The tide was out
and it was slippery on the shore. We had
a hard time but we pulled our canoe
past the high tide mark.

At midnight we arrived at Sakiassie's place. I knocked and at first there was no answer. I knocked again and my nephew Pudlat opened the door. Sakiassie and Pudlat and his son Elijah were there. Those people really welcomed us! They were so happy to see us they forgot to offer food! They only thought of it when I asked for some tobacco.

The next day they lent me a warm parka and took us home to Cape Dorset. When we came into our settlement and met the first people, I put up my hand and said, "It is me, Peter Pitseolak." They were so excited to see us alive; they had thought we were dead.

We came to my house and all my family
was there and so happy to see me they
all began crying! Suddenly our house was
full of people. I can't draw them all – there
were too many! I told them, ''We have
a helper we cannot see we know for sure.''

That's the story of how we came back
to Baffin Island and home to our wives
and children and grandchildren. The wind
brought us home when we had nothing
else to help us.

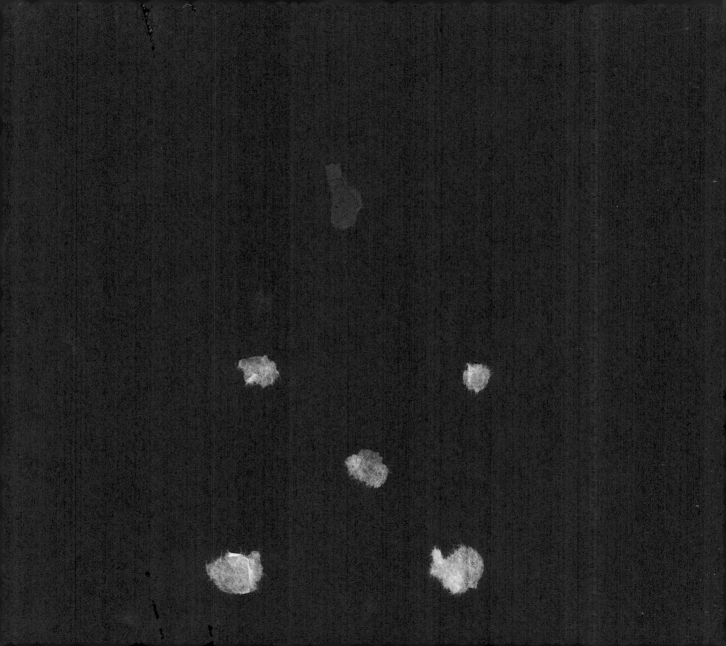